# If We Had a Lemon
# We'd Throw It
# and Call That the Sun

September 3, 2021

To Robert —
All the best to you and
your writing!

Warmly, Christopher

# If We Had a Lemon
# We'd Throw It
# and Call That the Sun

Christopher Citro

ELIXIR PRESS
DENVER, COLORADO

Book design by Steven Seighman
Cover photograph by Amanda Friedman

Library of Congress Cataloging-in-Publication Data

Names: Citro, Christopher, author.
Title: If we had a lemon we'd throw it and call that the sun / Christopher Citro.
Description: First edition. | Denver, Colorado : Elixir Press, 2021. |
"Winner of the Elixir Press Antivenom Poetry Award"-- Provided by publisher.
Identifiers: LCCN 2020030932 | ISBN 9781932418743 (paperback)
Classification: LCC PS3603.I898 I38 2021 | DDC 811/.6--dc23
LC record available at https://lccn.loc.gov/2020030932

ISBN: 978-1-932-41874-3

First edition: TK

10  9  8  7  6  5  4  3  2  1

# Contents

I

## II

*For Sarah*

Doesn't it make you happy,
driving the car through early fall,
with all these garages open. All these trampolines
in the yards.

On the next street, in the second headache
or the third headache, it's started to rain.

—John Gallaher, "The History of<br>Entanglements"

I

# It's Something People in Love Do

*We were happy and wretched and cloudy*
*and setting fire to everything for warmth.*

—Heather Christle, "Taxonomy of That November"

It's a late film, not one of their best, clogged
with a love interest that never really makes
your pants itch, but when the Marx Brothers
keep the train moving so the hero can make it
to town to record the deed and afford to marry
the girl of his dreams, they chop the whole
damn train up to feed the fire. Frightened
passengers in bustles and waistcoats watch
their seats axed from beneath them as women
cradle their children and men stand around
looking affronted. Then they hack up the walls
and the roofs, carrying armfuls of train forward
to turn into steam to keep things moving and
I'm not saying we should watch fewer old movies.
What I am saying is maybe everything's not
a metaphor for trying to pay the bills on time.
I love your credit score. It could pin my credit score
to the late summer soil and pee on its head.
My credit score would roll over and take it.
But what do you think of that chicken dinner
I made last night, how caramelized the thighs,
the bourbon from a plastic jug. How beautiful
that farmhouse looks passing by in the distance.
If we could get off this train we could go get it

and tear it to pieces with our teeth, tossing
hallways and lintels to the flames. Then we
could clean each other's face with our tongues.
It's called kissing. People in love do it.

# To the Dirt Which Will in Time Consume Us All

The camera pulls back to show a man running
down an empty city street. *Fin* appears white
across my chest. The camera keeps retreating,
revealing more. How would you like to go?
Last night—or was it two nights ago?—
I smashed a spider against my house with
my laptop lid. Some people say scientists
have proven traumatic memories get passed
down through DNA. I don't recall how,
something to do with being brutal to mice.
I love scientists. They're trying their hardest.
And they just want love. Whole schools of
photographers exist around expired film,
cheap plastic cameras with limitations,
scratches on the negatives. I love artists.
They're trying their hardest. And they just
want to be loved. Meanwhile, we live
in the side of a hill now. The house is ours
so the hill is our problem. Before we could
just drive by laughing, throwing beer cans
out the car window. Last weekend you took
a shovel and repaired the retaining wall—
I forget where that's at on my list, near the top
probably. I brought out cooling beverages
and took your picture when you were done,
the shovel already put away in the shed.
I went and got it back out, placed it in
your right glove. Stepped back. You tipped
your cowgirl hat and gave the subsiding hillside
the finger with your other glove, its cowhide
yellow like a star down in our yard.

# A Mud Puddle Shaped Mud Puddle

I waited for the stars to drop down,
a handful at least—is that too much to ask—
and spin a slight constellation in front of me.
I waited a long time. I'm still waiting.
Is it too much to ask for a willow to stop
its weeping when I float underneath
in my canoe with my incredibly fragile
happiness hanging out on the end of my
face for anyone to crush? Even a tree
that can't get its act together as a species.
I don't know about you people but I'm
tired of deciding what to do all the time.
Part of me wishes the anti free will folks
were right after all. I don't know about you,
but I know for a fact that I'm often about
twenty feet tall. I don't care what my
bones and muscles have to say about it.
There are summer nights I can stand
in the backyard and see right above
the cottonwoods. I can lean an elbow
on the power towers, feel constellations
in my hair stop spinning enough to pull
strands clean in their small wet mouths.

# So That's What an Invisible Barrier Looks Like

What kind of life is it where you're alive
on a Saturday morning alone in a room
with wonderful books, convinced any moment
someone's going to come through the door
and tell you someone you love has died?
Try locking the door! Then they can't get in.
See? Think these things through! There's
a roof above, some shingles and then
all the space anyone could ever need.
Out into the stars even. It just keeps going.
As far as anyone knows it just keeps going.
And last night when everyone was asleep,
convinced the mouse in the garage had climbed
a flight and made it into a kitchen cupboard,
you put your highball down and stood
in the kitchen with your head cocked
to one side like a private investigator would.
*When I said, I'd love to meet the private
investigator you hired, she said, You'd be
disappointed. She doesn't look like a private
investigator. And I looked at her on purpose
not saying anything.* It only took thirty seconds
walking around crouched over ear first to discover
that what had sounded like gnawing was actually
gears grinding in the coffee machine timer.
Every minute of every day it's back there
turning away just so we don't start crying
on the way to work. It's no kind of life to be
standing alone in a kitchen at two in the morning
with the only thing in your mind that
time passing close up sounds like a mouse

eating your kitchen and your drink's in the
other room, the quiet room with the soft
orange light, the couch and all the books.
Each one you can open up and get inside.

# We Might As Well Be Hovering

I admit it. I don't know what kind of stone
is underneath us all. I've lived years here
but it tends not to come up in conversation.
Somewhere people stand on pink quartz
when they stand in their backyards, pink
gins in each fist, a pink sunset pressed
against the sky. That's nice for them.
New York City would be squat if not
for the granite beneath all those fashionable
people and even the mole people who live
in the subways and have all-white eyes.
Here the grass does okay. Snowmelt
sinks through. There's a tallish building
every once in a while. Our cars are many
colored and so our children's small
electronic versions of cars. But what are
we really walking upon? A seed bank
in Norway holds a repository in case of
global catastrophe. Even North Korea
has a shelf. It's cold in Norway. The seeds
are buried deep inside a mountain.
When they dug out that rock someone
stopped to look at what was in her shovel.
Only three people in the world have a key.
I don't have one. I'm guessing you don't either.

# Shelter Awhile

*with lines borrowed from Mary Ruefle*

I'm not looking at the pines right now
because all I see are hands waving at me
and I'm not sure what that means. Yes,
I like the pines. I also like the wind.
I don't like being told what to do. I'll run
later today because I'll make myself.
It will be awful while it's happening
and I'll feel smug when I'm done.
I'll notice how the leaves look a little
different along the trail than they did
a week ago. That's how long it's been
since I last ran. Leave me alone.
We can read by the light of these
autumn full moons but it's my decision
what. *A bit of winding road.*
*The forest has drunk itself again*
*and reeks of pine.* The sky pale
as hospital sheets. Distant sounds
of planets like remembered arguments.
The last time I planted something
so long ago I'll plant my hands
beneath a big flat stone in the yard,
in the place a tree once stood.
I'll grow into a tree. I'll feel right for once.

## Smell of Wet Earth Like the Inside of My Hands

When I step outside I want the raindrops
pressing me a little deeper with each falling.
I might meet our spinning nickel center—
shining a dark light, wet overcoat of itself—
and I want the wild azalea above, to speak
one good sentence in my life worthy of
carving into a pine, one of those waiting
in an elementary school playground where
they still want the kids to have a tree so
they paved right up to the bark on that one.
I go to the drugstore sometimes just to
watch us. The hesitation in the ill-lit aisle—
who buys a loaf of bread at Rite Aid? I do.
You're waiting at home. You're hungry.

# One Push on Top Is All It Takes

I bought a membership to Costco
and a salad spinner and now I
don't know who I am anymore.
It helps me to think of my body
as a spaceship. I can understand
an engine room. Kidneys are
beyond me. Seeds in a tray
sprout long enough to grow
an inch or two then we rinse and
eat them on a salad or if we're
feeling frisky on a brie and ham
sandwich. If you reached down
and took the roof off this house
you'd see a human on the couch
worrying about things he has no
control over. We're just like anyone
else is what I mean. And someone's
got our roof in his hand. People
around here get sheets of red metal
up there. It costs a lot but never
needs replacing. Never in a human's
mouth means about 50 years.
After that who knows. This could
all be a wildlife preserve. A field
of feral romaine, a cloudy plastic
half sphere half rising from the soil.
It will be a sunny afternoon one day
thousands of years from now. I saw
my reflection in that curved surface
when I pulled it from the box. I cradled
the belly, the precise sort of emptiness
I could make some good use of.

# That's Why They Invented Cheesecake

The bush along the fence is a waterfall
of white blossoms again. So calm down.
You're like one of those fat spiders—
armored war machines that leap instead
of crawl—has gotten on your arm
just as you've picked up a wine glass
in each hand and there's nothing to do
but scream. We all have front doors.
The thing to do is go about your day
as if that's what you were planning
all along. When someone comes they'll
knock. Then you can put down what
you're doing and open up. Then you
can snap into one of those martial arts
crouches you've seen on TV and make
bullets ricochet with your wrists
with that keening whine that sounds
exactly as bad news going away should.
Don't lie in the lawn. Don't wait with
your mouth open. The several ways
of getting nourishment to your body—
one of your jobs each day since you
screwed up and grew up—do not
include just hoping it will wander in.
The bush is a riot of white blossoms.
That's now. At some point they'll be
gone. You won't remember the leaving.

# On a Foreign Planet Surrounded by Sugar Maples

The man I was at ten could take
a lightning bug from the air and write
a glowing arrow on my t-shirt
aimed at my spongy, wide open face.
The man I was then, smiling in the dark.
A summer night a thousand miles wide.
Little lights traversing the distances
at the height of our eyes, at the speed
of our hands. My head a spaceship
moving through it. My body a planet
running on another planet, stepping
on grass. When there was mud,
it stepped on mud. A blue spruce
against the stars. A house beside me
with lights, my room, my parents
alive watching reruns.

# Otherwise Inexplicable Animation to the Forms Above

Today I replaced the plastic sugar bowl with
a glass peanut butter jar so we don't get killed
by our sugar bowl. I can honestly say
my 18-year-old self could not have predicted this.
Air above the earth is measured in miles,
which is reassuring. Hermit crabs needing
larger shells gather in lines of decreasing sizes,
so when a new empty comes along each
hands their used down to the next smallest.
They hold on to one another while they wait.
The water is full of animals holding on to
one another. And when Picasso's sculptures
touch the earth at more than one point,
*each footing conveys a specific weight and*
*tension,* which means some like ballerinas,
some flatfooted, some the foundations of
tall buildings, some like a winter gnat resting
lighter than paper on paper or even hovering.
The reason authorities warn us when they're
going to test the emergency siren is because
some of us will spill coffee on ourselves
if we hear a wailing we're not expecting,
if the neighbors look at us in our window
the moment we happen to be looking out.

# Shadows of Blackbirds on Our Arms

The painters kept moving to places where
the light was better—France mostly—then
WW1 came and flubbed it all up. The story
begins with a man with the mind of a child
counting squares of light on the floor and
ends with that child, that floor, that counting.
When we stop to talk to coworkers no matter
what time of year we're not going to stay long.
We sort of take tiny steps toward our car
when the other person's talking. We act out
the adjective *antsy*. Sometimes when you're
hopping about in place I like to ask Do you
need to go to the bathroom? As if you're
a small child and I'm a big person. You're not
a small child. You have a t-shirt with a skull
but you look like a woman when you wear it.
For which I am thankful. I'm like a child
hopping up and down when I'm around you.
It's a field of sunflowers like someone painted
a lot of yellow across a canvas then smeared
the thick brushstrokes with a palm trying
to feel the stems and petals and the velvety
centers that turn scratchy in the autumn when
the light leaves us and all our heads begin to bow.

# Clocking Threats in the Local Environment

We walk hand in hand the backyard checking for nests.
They sneak in when we're not looking, opening wine bottles
Friday nights. A miniature buzzing thing—which smells
like chardonnay if you can get close enough—
passes the sliding doors, observes us inside sprawled
over the couch and living room floor like dead people,
continues along with its tiny mouthful of plant fiber
to bake one more warm curve of paper for the wall
of a new place to call home. Pointing at a cedar, I indicate
one we'd not seen before. Face high. It scarcely bears
imagining. Out of self defense I buy a can of Raid.
It sits in the garage still sealed in its grocery bag,
as I haven't the heart. Making the rounds last week,
like an open mouth with all its teeth removed, the nest
now empty. The old bees and the new bees we
almost think our own now flown off somewhere new,
the sort of place cruise ships port, we like to imagine.
That I espied yet another nest, large as my chest
when I take a deep breath, high up a cottonwood
along the back fence, revealed now by the lack of leaves,
is of no significance. That I called you away
from pointing at a rainbow to look at it likely is.

# In Small Significant Ways We're Horses

It's only as winter sets in, the whites of our eyes
roll forward, we see the lawn by staring at
the snow wishing we could see the lawn.
I never wish so hard I were a hang glider
as when I'm in a valley cleft by stones a giant
couldn't lift and I look into a wash of un-
differentiated blue. Cut a bat-shaped section
and replace it with me, aluminum wings,
and how right that would be. Did I mention
the hiking boots I'm wearing? I'll have a
sandwich or unpeel a granola bar from foil
which takes a sort of breath when I pierce
the seal. That's a lot to have happen just
to get a snack. I stared into a pot and you
know what, it did eventually boil so that's
one more thing they've been lying about
and sooner or later, ok later (let's hope)
when the sun's pooped it'll take a deep breath,
its lungs expanding past Mercury (a poison),
Venus (a lady), Mars (a bar), the gas giants
or thereabouts and did we miss earth getting
swallowed by sunlight, turning into one
of those clinkers you'd find along the tracks
you'd walk when you were little and did things
you wanted and this includes your backyard,
your boots, and get this all the granola bars
that have ever existed. Some people take fear
from this and go to bed quick. Some people take
anything goes, the sound of breath, the sweetness
of a golden raisin, the earthiness of rolled oats.

# Peaks Shot with Hairs of Lightning

Oatmeal and yogurt first thing. Fruit if there's fruit.
Leftover soup for lunch, those little bowties. You
in the yard last night explaining ten minutes the orzo
pasta in that day's lunch downtown. Me listening as
your fingers pinched air to show how pointy the ends.
The elephant above us breathing in slowly breathing
out even slower. A sky of spots forming along its skin,
yellow at first, like tar drops later. I looked them up
last summer and they're fungal but apparently harmless.
Did you have any soup or just the two salads? (I can
keep a conversation going.) I applied for a job yesterday.
I already have two jobs. We don't have to look
what year it is. The architect in the 70s mystery
had gold eyes and never opened his mouth very wide.
It worked great for a murderer. It would also work
for a cowboy. We drank too much wine with dinner
which we do sometimes because the world the world
the world. When you turned over in bed to try harder
to sleep I made to pull my hand from your breast
so as not to constrict you in your new position.
You used your other hand to stop me, to hold my hand
to you. I stayed right where I was as the blood began
to poorly circulate to that end of me. In my crime novel
the private investigator said something else about
drinking too much, smoke pouring out from
the mountains surrounding him called *Diablos*
in the book and probably in real life as well.

# To Keep At Least Partially in the Air

I can feel spring as a small painted blue stool
hovering behind to take me should I go.
I won't fall as far as the earth. I'll be startled,
but able to retain at least a little of my dignity.
In the winter, the stool's not there. Men travel
to Switzerland to throw themselves off peaks
in special suits like sugar glider squirrels—
passing through valleys, above fields so green
they sting the eyes—as we do in dreams.
It's so annoying I'm here with this blue stool.
You're there with your red stool. I can see it
in your eyes, in the way you look now
that it's warmed and each new bad idea
might not be bottomless. And the stories
of how cancer patients really die
that hardly anyone talks about or hears
because they're family stories or seen only
by professionals, can't get to us now.
They really can't. The dark pines aren't
looming over us. They're looking decorative
there at the corners of the yard. The impulse
to throw ourselves from the patio deck
because we're afraid of what will come
curls up and is blown from the wood slats
by the next warm breeze. After flying down
the side of the beautiful mountain, the man
using the special suit pulls a cord and floats
the last few hundred feet on a chute.
He doesn't look like a bird any more.
He looks like a man hanging from a rope—
several ropes—and bracing for the impact,
even if it's just a little one this time down.

# Anyway and Try to Stay Alive on What It Gives Us

The off-brand dollar store sticky notes adhere
to each other great to anything else in this world
less great. Like us. Sometimes it feels like
the back of a big box store in here (my head)
when you walk up to that wall of TVs all
showing the same scenes. It's huge but it's also
lots of little not huge things. You know how
we sound like idiots when we try to say
important things. Well, me at least. Going
shopping together is like living our lives
together. Please don't tell me about how
they sprayed to kill mosquitoes forgetting
to warn the beekeepers and the bodies are
so high the numbers themselves look obscene.
All those zeroes. All those empty holes in
the honeycomb. I'm going to lose it next to
the mustard with a label just like a leading
national brand. Until you look closely that is.
There are words there but not the ones we need.

# Beaver Lake

Sometimes you squash a bug and you're left
with just bug. Slightly flatter or crimped.
Other times you squash one and it's applesauce
applesauce everywhere. There's a book
across the table I'm going to ignore now
for the next say two hundred years or so
because there's no way I'm going to look
at that mess again. Plus it's green. Cripes.
Maintain my new found running regimen
and my legs hurt every day. Let it lapse—
as I have of late—and everything else
hurts. What's fun about being yourself?
The German deli sells bologna that actually
gets you excited about bologna. It's that good.
There's supposed to be a blood moon tonight—
which is just a full moon—and I'm excited
to see it. Last night I stood on the deck
looking at the thing and thought, *Tonight*
*you're not special. Tomorrow, you'll be special.*
The bug juice has seeped into the book cover,
dried and warped it a little. I just let myself
look. I'll use Windex to wipe it later because
ammonia kills germs. I've done this before.
I have a plan. Later when I drive to the park
to run around the geese, I'll pass the farm
where they've carved the corn maze already.
I'll think about stopping, then remember it's
for kids. The pumpkins with their faces
painted on smile at you in the day and at night
change back to just regular pumpkins.

# One Light in a Field of Other Lights

I never buy fireworks because they're just
too much. The future is approaching, and
I'm afraid. Then it's gone, and I'm like,
What happened? The neighbors have finally
opened their pool. The summer's half over.
Their long-limbed daughters are slapping
against the surface. The hemlock's in the way.
All I can hear is the slapping. The blue sky
and show of clouds are reflected in this glass
deck table. A girl throws herself in the air
and lands on the sky, obliterating it. Perfectly.
And when we turned onto our street last night,
I said, Oh look, gesturing toward explosions
in the sky above the minor league stadium.
Two people in the car went, Oh, and continued
talking. Bicycling far from home, one fell
sick from the heat. A stranger mowing
flagged another stranger driving by who
gave them a lift into town in his pickup.
They were able to figure out what to do
from there. Every little plane in the sky—
especially at night—I want to reach up and
give a little push to help it on its way.

# Our Beautiful Life When It's Filled With Shrieks

I'm doing a balancing act with a stack of fresh fruit
in my basket. I love you. I want us both to eat well.
We're not allowed to buy blackberries anymore
because they're mean to their workers and you
read leftwing news sites. Till when? I asked and you
said nothing. So that's one healthy food off the list.
I'm still buying pineapples and you're still eating them.
I guess you've never seen the websites about those.
Nobody in this supermarket knows that I am a puma.
This morning our cat rolled on the floor showing me
her belly which I leaned down and rubbed.
Beneath a backyard pine tree the neighbor's cat
was eating one of our cat's moles—at least the moles
we rent from the landlord for her. It's so complicated
staying alive sometimes. The voices of the collection
agencies on the answering machine sound menacing.
They're paid to sound that way and they're not paid
much more than the people they're menacing,
which can get you thinking if you're the sort
who likes to think about that sort of thing.
Other people subscribe to adventure cycling
magazines and read about men who rode across
Turkey in the late 1800s before anything was
happening in the world. Before cantaloupes
probably existed. When you could get an honest
wage for an honest day's blackberries. When we
loved like fierce mountain storms, with the blood
of eagles in our hearts, exchanging grocery lists
that just said *you you you you* all the way down.

# At First It Buzzed Then Even the Buzzing Stopped

The sky eventually snaps off, drifts.
You can eat a sandwich from a book,
if the cover's glossy and unstained.
Clean things look clean. If something
looks clean, proceed as if it were.
You're like all the pre-Socratics
wrapped up into one lumpy human
with saggy shorts, wondering if
there's enough rotisserie chicken
left to make a breakfast or if we
should just fry eggs. Hold an egg
to the window when the sun's out.
Two different things, really.
The list of your achievements runs on.
Teeth cleaning. Finding a better job.
Affording firewood when winter falls
again like a hug from a drunk friend
you wish would just leave you
the hell alone. And somewhere
a child has fashioned a one-string guitar
from a shovel and flattened tin cans.
How can I fix this garbage disposal
I dropped a quarter in two years ago?
I switched it on to see if that would help.
It didn't. A star just switched on
at the edge of a collapsing dust cloud.
Life is what happens during
the period between birth and death.
Thank you, scientists, that's a big help.

# Go On Take Another Little Piece of My Heart

One of the reasons I'm loathe in general to crack
the bedroom door and scurry many-legged out
is hearing praying mantises were never endangered.
That's a lie and mythy. Clunk there goes another
long drawer of my youth. If you can't believe
what a kid two years older who lives down
the road tells you then who can you believe?
Next they'll say swallowing a watermelon seed
won't get you pregnant. I'll stay rather in bed,
one foot in eight years old and the other outside
the covers for heat regulation. In my dream
I'll have built a mansion with well-lit staircases
so never at the top will I step where there's no step—
slapping a Frankenstein foot too hard on nothing
and feeling an animal shame. You can go to jail
for eating an owl. Stick a hand out a car window
and it'll get cut off. An ancient Greek was the last
person to have known all there was to know. Or
maybe it was someone medieval in a cold monastery
surrounded by the dark hoards with their drinking
and folk songs and rumpy-pumpy. How would he
know he knew everything? And if it's just something
we made up why do we need so to build our monster
in our image? The monks named their arguments
the names of women because they were monks
and men without women. Three A propositions
(All X is Y) in a row was Barbara. Hello, Barbara!
In a hard cell on a night lasting several hundred years,
a monk hunkers down on a straw mat. No one knocks
at the door but the wind with everything behind it.

# The Sweet of Being Made Right

I've come outside with the knots in my skull
to see what the spring sunlight can do. I look
at the grass pressed pale. I see some dirt clods
that shouldn't be there. Some animal that tunnels
for a living pushed that up below the snow.
Someone planted evergreens precisely there
to look good from the east windows—except for
the bedroom shaded by cedars so strangers can't
witness the lovemaking or the solitary weeping.
And that's nice. This sunlight that gets all over
everything is nice. It's been a long winter.
The yard hasn't slept for days. It's pale and shaky.
It needs a plate of sausages and tomatoes.
I need a plate of sausages and tomatoes.
I've come outside and everything's flowing
into and out of my head, which I guess is
what I wanted. That fly that's so black
it looks sticky, that fly landed on my arm
and didn't know enough to fly away when
I jerked. It's a new world and we're new in it.
Even these scars are new—the scars in the lawn
and the ones on my arm, little strings that look
like bows the further away from us you get.

# I'm Back Here I'm Paddling Too

First atoms. Then the electron. Now we
have to deal with quarks, flavors, charms,
and I can't seem to keep up with the dirty dishes.
And we have a dishwasher. Last night at 2 a.m.
I stood up and I didn't know what to do next
(downstairs a library). One good thing
about summer is going outside and looking
at the sky equals doing something. You probably
thought I was having one of my moments
when the cord doesn't quite reach the outlet,
but it took me so long to get in the Toyota
because a balloon I think. Anyway a silver dot
above downtown. Too early to see a star.
I think it just revolved. I'm looking for a string.
I touch the persimmon or I do not depending
on whim or something deeper and unavailable.
Every wave you see the result of complex
forces working via cause and effect to end
in the random crashing we need now and then.
Switch off the internal news feed long enough
to remember to breathe and then actually do it.
One deep one has a measurable effect on
the nervous system. Take it with me now.
Slowly in. Slowly out. Those vines along the wall
look like rivers. You lift the paddle from
the sticky water, place it in again and push.

# Dear Diary Where Is Everybody

Since we packed up and moved this summer—oh
what joy, what rapture—my left elbow won't stop
hurting. The cat just rubbed against it and I felt
a deep soreness with a soft wonderfulness on top.
It didn't make the pain go away. They stayed
together and my brain took a subterranean voyage
like when you read a fairy tale that's disgusting
and beautiful, the way they used to be and
the good ones still are. Most satellite dishes
point south, he told me standing below several
pointing north. One faced west. I didn't have
the heart to say anything. When I left this time
I actually called back to the kids, Don't grow up
too fast! One of them—our favorite—had drawn
a dragon for you. Does she want it with fire
shooting out? she asked. You bet your ass,
I said—but not in those words. I texted you
the photo right then, with her little arm across
the top edge, obscuring a second unfinished
dragon she didn't want to spoil the good one.
What I'm trying to tell you is *plant*. Plant
the bulbs if you want to. I don't have a bulb
plan in my head other than come spring
a miniature circus of colorful membranes
beside our door. Folks who visit should know
the kind of people we are and get pollen on
themselves. Over drinks later you and I will pick
each gold speck off their arms with our eyelashes.

## Gathering a Few Facts

It's enough on this Monday morning that I can
remember the difference between a thorn
and a prickle and it appears as if I'll actually be
getting to work on time. It's the same time
as it always is in this parking garage,
sodium lamp time, who's walking suspiciously
behind the car time, what would I do if
someone put a gun in through my window time.
Can a travel mug of hot tea work as a
weapon of self defense? I know I wouldn't
want any poured on me, but then again
I'm not a criminal. I'm soft. A true thorn
is a modified branch and a prickle is something
to do with the skin only. Most roses have
prickles not thorns, which is disappointing
on so many levels and the kind of thing I have
to carry around with me as well as manage
morning traffic. I'm keeping it together.
I'm not harassing other people in their cars.
I see us, many of us, sitting behind the wheel
for a moment or two, gathering one or two
firm facts to ourselves before gritting our teeth
and stepping onto the streets where nobody loves us.

# You're Welcome to the Rest

I will have you fiercely in the forefront of my
thoughts for the eight hours a day I'm paid to.
The rest of my time is mine. If I want to notice
oak leaves in rainwater, that's for me, not for you.
I love it when it's stormy here in the city because
as the sky darkens the rooms in the tall buildings
light up so anyone can see in—about as well as
a three inch man on my toes could see into my chest,
but still I make out a few things. A houseplant
someone must care for over and above
their hourly duties. I saw a couch once—I think
it was in a bank, seven or eight stories up there
closer to the clouds. And a tungsten lamp, forty watts
I imagined, dropping a very human halo of orange
onto one end. In my mind I hummed to myself
riding a strange elevator noiselessly up, excuse
me, pardon me, until I'd found that room and
that couch. The office's occupant leaving me
quite alone, going on with her business, clicking
a mouse and understanding. The feeling of my bones
stretching out along its soft expanse, my forehead
warmed in that amber glow so many feet
above the street—that feeling belongs to me.

# You Can Keep Your Employee of the Month Award

I need to work out a way to keep my rowboat with me
even at work. Double the amount of productivity
you expect me to crank out? Sure, if I can do it
standing in my rowboat, looking off into the distance
for a heron nest inside the cottonwoods. Am I working
quickly enough? Let me know when you get the chance.
I'll be floating along the shore watching midges
form new constellations against a sky so blue
it makes your eyes squeak. I'm going to have to
clock in at the start of my day and clock out before
leaving. Just make sure the button can be operated
by one end of an oar, with me holding onto the other,
leaning out of—but still firmly seated in—my rowboat.
*Dreaming of Lime Trees* is the name I've just decided
my boat will be called. I'm probably a thousand miles
from the nearest lime tree, but the sparkling water
I just sipped is lime flavored and that got me thinking.
You'd never accept that sort of nonlinear thinking
from an employee, but I did it on my break, paddling out
toward the open water, enjoying my muscles waking up
inside my shirt, the tang of fresh air forcing its way
into my nostrils. In fifteen minutes I'll be back—I know
you find that hard to believe—at my desk in my chair
at my computer with my eyes doing what you pay me
to have them do. I will. And when I wobble a little,
it's because a rowboat in an office is going to wobble a little.

# We Come Here Every Day So You've Already Won

I think anyone who works here should be allowed
to go up to the roof whenever she wants.
It's only ten floors and we're certainly all adults.
To stand on top of the office with both our feet
planted firmly on its forehead, with nothing
on our foreheads but the big stupid sky. The white sky.
The blank stare sky. They sky that won't help
buy groceries. The sky we can't live in. The sky
that doesn't keep us warm at night, that isn't a place
to go to when the work day's done and everyone
shoots out the building's mouth heading home
or maybe to a treadmill to try to keep from dying
or to a bar to try to keep from dying. Imagine
how good that would feel. We might jump up
and down a little but we're not going to hurt
the building. It's stronger than we are. That's
obvious at this stage. We're not going to harm
the sky being so close to it. The sky will just
back away to leave us more alone. Resigned
to this, we're certainly not going to throw our
frail bodies from the stone edge. We're not
hunched at our terminals all afternoon picturing
how we'll look reaching into air either side with
the sore, bird-like claws our hands have become.

# Returning Home After the Funeral

There's a handprint on my chest in the shape of a hand.
It comforts me to find it there. I move through the house
calmly, telling myself to let whatever happens happen.
If I open a cupboard door to check the saltines are still there—
and they are—I'll take that for what it is. If part of the flap
sticks out and makes the door difficult to close, then that's
what's happening at that point in time and space. Spring
is on the verge outside. Small black birds sprinkled across
the tired snow, as if each one hangs by a long hair from
a marionette's frame. It's raised in the sky and the birds
rise at different intervals. It moves to the neighbor's yard
and lowers, the birds drop here, there, investigate the cold
with their feet and faces. I've made several circuits of
the upper floor and the handprint on my chest is still there.
I checked in a mirror as I passed the bathroom the last time.
Through the closed kitchen window I can hear a train whistle.

# The People Who Live Near Us Are Our Neighbors

Two doors down the neighbor kid hung
a white wire reindeer with twinkle lights
from a tree as if freshly shot and ready
for butchery. It's pleasing to live so near
the country, the trees, the rolling hills
and apple stands. But it does mean
you have to put up with gun shots
into the scrub land on winter evenings.
Some nights there's a patrol car parked
out front. We wish him and his family
the best. We eat popcorn because it's
all natural and sort of old fashioned
and brings us a little closer to the life
of the soil. The life of the soil is nearby,
past the gas station on 57, up the road
from the dog park, across the intersection
from where the guy lost control
and slammed into a mother of three.
He was driving to McDonalds. It said
that on the news report. He'd smoked
the heroin just before heading out for
his Tuesday dinner. His little silver
cloud rising above us all, the dead
reindeer made of lights, the popcorn,
the gradual inconsistencies and the fields
someone still plows and tends and pulls
pumpkins from when the morning
dew gives gradually way to frost.

## The Sky We Want to Reach Up and Press Our Thumbs Into

Enough to see the indentations float away.
We were here. This is what it felt like.
Our dreams were often unsettling but
we took solace from the latest science
saying to have any is the benefit, inner
corridors swept clean by night winds—
no matter if you're on stage singing to
versions of yourself below or standing
in a field wedding-dressed with snakes,
coils dripping from your arms replaced
with others as they fall. Those are some
powerful snakes. These wounds in the trees
have been put there, some by hand, some
flames from the sky. Last thing before
you crawled into sleep you told me I am
the man you are glad that you love—
you said it much better—and I got up
on one elbow and looked while you said it.
So many hot dark little boxes snapping shut.
The night quieting down to a livable size.

# Bring Me with You

*And I saw the sea lifting up and shining like a blade with the sun on it.*
*And high up, in the icy wind, an aeroplane flew toward us from the land.*

—D.H. Lawrence, Letter to Lady Cynthia Asquith, Sunday Jan 30, 1915

I looked at my ass in the large living room mirror this morning
and thought Youth has left me spinning slowly to a stop
in the mud rut of a country road on the way to someplace
locals dump dead refrigerators. I need to stop talking
to myself and start exercising more. We begin by finding
the power walkers unbelievably silly and end by wondering
where we could get away with it without our friends seeing.
I love the woman I sleep with every night, and I take this moment
to thank her for all she does. On hot nights we barely touch
but there's always some small part that does, a kneecap pressed
along a thigh, the bottom of a foot against the top of a big toe.
In the morning I invariably wake up with my arms around her.
If I were trying to save her from drowning, I'd grab her
the same way. I'd lay flat and let her use me for a raft,
the waves slopping up the side of my body. She sitting
with her knees up under her chin, one hand above her eyes
scanning the horizon. The other steadying herself on my ass.

# Sick of Sick

In the future we ended up getting
our colds last weeks and weeks.
We spend glamorous Saturdays
coughing at the arm of the couch,
flinching at the thought of someone
touching our midsection. The bugs
get stronger and we look like dogs
wandering wet streets, seeking shelter.
Anyways that's how it feels today.
I can hear you coughing from another
room. Remember how July felt?
I stopped myself in a moment then,
thought Don't take it for granted.
I forget what I went and did after that,
but confound it if four months later,
with windows shut and the furnace on,
if I don't feel as if I went ahead and
took it for granted. When will I learn?
We've bought so much cold medicine
we're probably on some sort of registry.
The kid at the store doesn't even ask
for our IDs anymore. He just rings
the stuff up and gives us that look.
Do I make myself cough while swiping
my debit card, even if I don't have to
cough just then? Yes, I'll admit I do.
Does it get me anywhere? No, it does not.
My brain is muddled with mucus.
Every day is the same as the last.
Some of them I drag myself to work
anyway. The rest I nurse myself.

I want to be hot rodding, drunk driving
golf carts into hot midnight reservoirs,
having sex in inappropriate locations,
but I'm nursing myself instead.
Let's both get better so we can
have sex in inappropriate places.
We'll follow that checkout clerk home
and do it on the hood of his car
while the engine's still warm and
the ticking of cooling strong metals.

# An Emergency Every Day of the Week

It's how you know I love you,
the trees along the ridgeline
sway into one another
the way I lean into you.
Clouds rush from us
the way we run away from
the world. An ambulance
screams along the street
at 3 a.m. Inside there's
you on a gurney and me
on a gurney. No nurses
either side, not even a driver.
We split the cold air like
a scalpel. A bump. I reach out
my hand for yours. Yours
is there in the air and it
clasps mine. The ambulance
just went off a cliff.
Now we're flying
and we're fine.

II

# The Mutual Building

The new café is pleasant though cluttered
by all the men and women attracted by
low priced coffee, who when grabbed
release their tails and flee. There's snow
everywhere. When is someone going
to come clean this up? If you look up
at the top of the tallest building, first
you'll see a star—which is lit up at night
and nice—then you'll see some numbers.
The first ones are the temperature, which
is fine. (Pigeons stay all through the winter,
walk right in front of you along the ice.
They get in your way, but it's fine.)
The second is the time and—here's
the spiky thing—it's always wrong.
No one seems to notice but secretly
everyone knows and everyone keeps
looking up then feeling bad inside.
No one needs the wrong time in the sky
when we're just trying to cross the street.
A city parking enforcement van says it
Makes frequent stops Do not tailgate and
even the little bundles of baby being
pushed through the slush by women
with no hats on their hair are thinking
I thought you weren't supposed to
tailgate anyone in the first place. Now
what am I supposed to think? Which is fine.
Each day at 5:30 the man with the bedroll
stands in the crook of the bank building
directly above the heat exhaust. The first day

he said Any spare change? The second day
he just stood there with his hand out.
It had a mitten on the end. The mitten
was a light beige, the same color nearly
as the stones in the side of the bank.
But that's not the bank's fault. The next
day he won't even have his hand out.
The day after that it's entirely likely
he'll become a statue and that's how
banks get the lions they have out front.

# How We Make It Home Eventually

*. . . and ring like crystal in the trees.*

—Charles Wright

I could be lost in the arctic at this moment,
leaning to eat the last of the leather from my shoes,
eyeing my friend sitting on his pack at my feet,
cupping hands to his face and trying not to cough
for the energy it takes. Outside us a sharp wind,
and there's nothing but white, a blankness we cannot eat,
a nothing that will hollow us out with bladed breath
until we stand spinning, a thin line
separating inside from out. Another gust and we topple,
a last tinkling sound sliding away to any shore.

# Save the Receipts for a Kind of Diary

We bought more cutlery so our cutlery
drawer is full all the time now.
I can't believe we waited so long
to feel so good. You never notice people
blowing up beach balls. You only ever
just see the beach balls. A bird falls
out of a tree now and then in spring,
received by waiting cats and dogs,
so we rarely chance to come upon it.
Our dog leaps into our lap to lick our face.
We pat the shiny fur where the cat
has licked herself after stepping
from the pine shadows. Most strip
malls are built on the sites of former
wilderness. Then again, you can
say that about anywhere, really.
When you bought me the reflective
vest for my new jogging hobby,
I didn't have the heart to say thanks
but there's no way I'd ever wear
that thing in public. Now the streets
are dark, I'm careful the self-adhesive
straps hold it firmly to my chest
as I run into traffic hoping not to
be killed. I make sure the blinking
light you bought for the back is
going so people behind can see
where I am. Anyone in front has
my big frightened face, the air
almost visible as it's pulled like

ropes down my ribcage and coiled
along creaking shelves for a long
voyage then yanked out and
expelled every few seconds.

# Show Me Around This World of Yours

Studded snow tires spun all these little roses
into the driveway sealant on your three-point
turns to head to work this winter. You pointed
where a deer pulled the sprouting tulip bulb
clean from the earth. It lay on its side like someone
trying to reach a seat belt in economy. I
thanked you for pointing it out and set it up
right back in the hole. Move on. Perhaps
we should rethink our relationship to pastel.
Some planes when they pass sound as if they'll
tear our heads off. I can feel that way watching
you cross the floor on your way to put your
fingers in my mouth. Those oranges were
unusually juicy and sweet. We sang the
description to one another spontaneously.
Yes make an appointment to have that mole
looked at. Odds are I'll live through today
but what I'll have accomplished by bed
will hardly seem worth it. Have you walked
through a museum lately? The mattress ads
say we spend a third of our lives on them.
Sorry as I am at such moments I can feel
the weight of this entire house. No one's
asking me to lift it from the foundation,
cup it in my hands like it's a sick bird or
something. Mash earthworms in my mouth
to lower in through one of those tubes in the roof
we still don't know the purpose of. We warbled
when we said how good the oranges were,
and we both had them in our mouths,
our fingers pulling them apart as we sang.

# Bats and Applesauce

On the deck at one in the morning, no less than
three swing between me and the patio doors.
I say nothing into the phone because I don't want
to alarm you. Hanging from the legs upside down
might cure your bad back. Who am I to say?
I think something's safe if it doesn't taste bitter.
That's the level I'm working at. And fiddlehead
ferns are carcinogenic and delicious. A primary
component of bibimbap. Maybe the cause for
elevated stomach cancer rates in Korea. Plus
the fronds at some point contain cyanide. Face it.
This is a plant that does not want to be eaten.
It's been around long enough to know what it
wants and how to get it. Like a pop singer, we
respond more to the attitude than to the tune
which floats away on the next warm breeze.
When you're small, you eat what's set before you.
Later you can choose, and though friends may
feel bad inside for you munching a veggie burger
at the smoky BBQ, it's your life. At the last, well,
what comes down the tube goes in whether
you like it or not. Milk at either end. Or milk
substitute. Hospitals find themselves located
in the poorest parts of cities because the taxes
are cheapest. So you look out the windows you
can't open and see someone on the sidewalk
standing in the sun on a weekday afternoon.
He might be a criminal, or he might simply have
no money and no place to go. How beautiful
he looks. The cup of pale applesauce on a tray.
The curtains you can't reach to pull. We're
surrounded by things that will swoop down on us.

# Barely Managing the House Plants Thing

I refuse to give up on the majesty palm
everyone says I was a sucker for buying.
You get what you pay for, they say and I say
I paid ten bucks and they start to smile and
I lean in ready to nip at them. I'm like a terrier
for my peeps. The protective instinct. I can't
make the sun shine out of my face though.
It's cold and we're north and the sun is a jerk.
And this isn't July. The majesty palm and I
just have to make it to July. I picture myself
and the plant on the deck buzzing with heat,
waving our fronds in almost tropical breezes.
I clipped off four whole branches this morning
because there's no coming back to life once
you're that yellow and crinkly. Someone said
it was a marketing scam. They live on riversides
in Madagascar, are cultivated in Florida by con artists,
then sold for cheap to chumps in box stores
thinking they're getting a deal when all they're getting
is a slow demise no matter what. Someone said
mist, so now I mist. Imagining my home
a 1970s smooth pad with one of those egg chairs,
cocaine on the coffee table and thick green palms
in a corner, at least I could start with the palm part.
The 1970s lasted two weeks, then the 80s set in
and death began its new wave lapping up the stalk.
I'm not giving up though. Someone said talk to them.
So when the cat's asleep, I approach a frond and speak
into its green microphone. I love you. I say, don't die.
I'm sorry this isn't Madagascar, the 1970s or July.

# Yesterday I Saw a Small Snake Holding Still

The light, the light flowing inside the light,
the songbirds starting out from under
wild-haired bushes yet to flower as
spring heaves its thighs onto summer.
The maintenance of the sky, always up
there, better than us, clearer, or angry
green and lowering on little tubes that
suck our ranch houses off the crust when
(here's a lie that's a wish) all it wants
is to taste us, lick the mechanical aspects
of our lives. Hello ant. How's your corner
of the farm today. Pressed between
two sheets of shatterproof glass. How's
yours? It feels like we're at the beach
just because of the humidity. I find it
hard to work computers too. These
sensory apparatus aren't keeping up.
That sound from the forest, a buck's
six-point rack clacking against the
junk trees on the hill. Even calling them
*junk trees* makes me feel bad about myself.
And they are junk trees—any landscaper
will tell you that then return to mowing
and her cigarette. Lawns serve no useful
purpose but beauty and we love them.
They're poisoning our water but we love them.

# Holding My Head in Both My Hands

Look, if I was the kind of person who could
become satisfied by a few earthenware pots
with cacti and golden mums on the porch
don't you think I'd have owned a few by now?
I'm not incapable of taking care of myself.
I eat popcorn when I want to eat popcorn—
but it's not as simple as that most of the time.
You don't see the same birds on the same
branches day after day. The sun doesn't live
lodged in one willow crevice until it burns
the green away. We move—or I move—
because this was working at one point and
now it's not. I imagine the first thing
the astronauts think when pulled free of
the atmosphere is how good a beer and a
folding chair on the edge of a reservoir
would be just then. The doorway to all
the stars that have ever been just the other side
of their skulls and each one turning, raising
a camera to focus back in on the earth.

# Elegy for the Travel Agents

It might be easier to look at photographs of a lake
than to actually plan, prepare and take a vacation,
but sometimes you have to find a tablet somewhere
and start a list. Look at the sun. It's not a telephone
that keeps ringing. One word written with conviction,
such as *must*, is like taking a step on a wide, frozen
lake when waves are singing along the shoreline.
Sometimes the waves are inside you. Your chest
for instance, each nipple a wolf nose pushing out
towards what you might do next. You need a vacation.
You know you do. And the need's so acute it's
getting in the way of making it happen. Welcome to
the way most people walk down the sidewalk each day.
Welcome to those above ground pools you buy
for a couple hundred bucks then fill with hose water
and sit in in your backyard as the sides slough
slowly out of shape and dark hawks stitch the surface
with moving shadows. You look for a place
to set your drink protected with its own umbrella
and there is no place. Your drink looks up at you—
stares up at you, really. Your drink two weeks
in the Bahamas. You tilt the umbrella to cover
the ice cubes, to keep them alive a little longer.

# I Was There My Feet Were Wet and I Looked Up

I have literally no idea what you're
talking about and when I say *literally*
I mean I have a basic idea but what
do you want me to think about *you*
and how do I feel about what that says
about *me* and how long our sentences
grow even when it's just something
about cherry tomatoes, no I don't
think I saw the Milky Way any better
at the beach than our backyard but
I was there my feet were wet and I
looked up. Other people sleep through
the night or they don't. People don't
talk about it. Or they do. A woman
at work said I like coming here because
it gets me out of the house. And we
wish upon a star. Those recordings
they place in the news once a year,
what light sounds like, how the galaxy
breathes to a microphone, and it's all
some version of static and standing
too close to a bookshelf on thick carpet.
A tilt that reads you and boo goes the
world beneath your feet. That so much
of my well-being should depend on
my inner ear said you one night in bed—
we do other things than talk—with
an opened mouth at how thin the sheets
around us. On some we write window.
On some to do. On some please help me
move this. I need you. I saw the fawns
this morning tearing at the panicgrass.

# If We Had a Lemon We'd Throw It and Call That the Sun

*and that was one thing quickly becoming another*

—Gerald Stern, "Red Wool Bathrobe"

I'd like to invite you to the party but I don't
know your name, have your address, or
know you well enough to really want you
around my cat. I feel a kinship with all people
and then I share a beach with them and want
to yell use your inside voice. We're outside
but that doesn't mean we'll not dissolve
if raised to the light. Some days the sea wants
to chew us into shattered two-by-fours.
Some days she's a kitten pasting soft hairs
around our ankles. I know—I know this for
a fact—there are moist pasta salads being
prepared and eaten all around me—in those
bushes for instance—and I'm not getting any.
I tried to start my life out right and still
lost track of where I was going. Example,
I picked my college because my girlfriend
went there. She slept with my best friend.
I went there anyway. That determined
the course of the rest of my life. I wiped
the table down with bleach before sitting
and now my forearm smells. It's going
to be okay though. I'm going to need this
bleach-arm for some purpose. To identify
some wanderers in the sky it's helpful to
determine the color. At a distance everything

for me goes gray. A mountain range in
a black-and-white film. We've been walking,
my horse and I, for days. For water we
think about rivers and lick our own ideas.

## The Hay Out There and the Hay in You

The way you want it is—
you hope to be flying
then realize you are flying.
I've eaten blackberries
from your hand where
they're warm from July
and your hand. I wonder
when I wake in morning—
am I afraid as usual or
do I feel nothing. I try
to keep myself safe as
I begin to move about.
Were my knees always
numb on the outside
like that. Will I recognize
when my brain contracts,
desiccates like nut meat
turning sour. Guess what—
it's begun to rain. You've
been getting wet—and
you've been crying a little—
but the light moving across
the distant fields. The light
riding the distant fields.

# The Low Crumble of Distant Applause

In this new house we're visited regularly by giants.
Some explanation. The giants, for one, are very small.
At least that is how they appear to us—so close to the sky,
etched against blue folded into clouds. And by visit
I mean, of course, watched over. But it can feel like
a visitation when, for instance, you are standing
on the red deck high above the lawn waking up,
and your new haircut flutters in the breeze.
From inside the kitchen, standing above greasy water,
I look through the screen and see you—frightening
in your precisely defined beauty, your white shirt
a sail catching and flinging back the sun and wind,
through this window screen, through the thin bone of
my forehead. And through the mile of heavy air
above us where the miniature people eating peanuts
look down and feel glad because of a fleck of light
against the red and green and do not even know
why. I know why.

# We Live on a Foreign Planet This One

It's sunlight eventually. They figured this out
long ago. The flame on the candle. It all ties in.
The trick to relaxing is to accept yourself.
After all you can't be that bad can you?
Just talk together with friends. Don't also sit
on top of your head listening to everything
you say and second guessing it right then,
later that night, and here and there the next day.
If a good day is simply a state of mind, then
stand naked in your front windows, wave hello
to the snow crusts along the drive and resolve
to improve. Physically first if you feel up to it.
We built a sort of little gym in the basement
next to the cat box. We let go drops of sweat
which fall onto the concrete which hasn't seen
the elements since this house was built umpteen
years ago. They come from the food we eat,
the wine and seltzer and tea we drink. They
come from rain and the sea before that. They
come from clouds and those little puffs you see
from people's faces when the mercury drops
and the air outside our houses wants to kill us.

# Waves Frozen Like Wrinkles on Dog Skin

A second or so for humans. That's our delay.
The world could cough out of existence
and none of us would know for a second.
We'd go on chopping kale as if it still existed.
The flies catching on first, remaining mum.
This is how it ends—us staring at the flies
wondering what their problem is. Custard pie.
Ginger snaps. Sweet tea. A bowl of ice cream.
Your bright eyes. I'm listing what's going away.
The last time we spoke I said *I love you* twice.
Once because I do. Again to see if you did too.
Phones nowadays don't click when we hang up
but should. The silence after the after-silence
deafening. The kitchen clock ticks like soldier
feet on a bridge, the kind made from grating.
It's holding us up but we can see right through.

# Creation Myth

Overgrown weeds had hidden the car until
the brushfire revealed it. Once the doors cooled,
neighborhood kids came to investigate. One rubbed
a circle clear with his sleeve and clicked his glasses
against the window. A beautiful woman lay
against the seat—black dress, sparkles
around her neck, confetti in her hair.
Next to her sat a man in a tuxedo,
a noisemaker stuck out of his lapel
where there was also a flower—his face toward
the woman, and each of their eyes were closed.
One of the boys banged on the hood to see
if that would do anything. Timmy saw
the man open his eyes without moving his head.
He saw the woman and smiled. The moment he did,
she opened her eyes and smiled. They turned,
he started the car, she adjusted a dress strap,
and the car exploded to life. It leapt from the ash pile,
just missing the boy who'd slammed on the hood.
Timmy, having jumped back, watched it
run through the field, up to the road and away.
Later, as a grown man, he'd sometimes
think of the woman, the way she looked straight
ahead as she reached to her shoulder, sliding
the black strap up and over, and when
he walked his feet barely pressed the ground.

# Light at the Beach a Thousand Doctors

We've been to the beautiful place and seen
what the beautiful people were doing and
tried to join in the best we could. The sun
fell against the sea and a hundred hands rose
to lift it into the sky again. The hands supple,
touchingly small against an ample underbelly
all yellow and hot and broadcasting. Evenings
birds lowered from clouds to drop morsels
of warm food into our upturned mouths.
Washed down with sips of ice-chilled wine
the color of bees. Nearby fences high,
made with exotic bushes and steel wires.
We played no music nor listened to any
because we were music and clapped as
the sun set when it was supposed to. I lie.
The sun clapped for us. Later in our alone
place, I rubbed green gels into your belly.
Careful not to press myself into your pain,
I blew cool air from my sky-like cheeks,
looking like a god in a painting then. You
looked like yourself. The air conditioning
clicked on like a child telling a beautiful lie
to another child in another room of the house.

# Removing the Butter Dish from the Fridge with a Sense of Urgency

Because the neighbor closed his pool on Labor Day
when it was 92 degrees, it's now 56 two days later.
You bet I blame the guy. Some people I love but
they're no good for me so I leave them alone.
I think of them from time to time, when the weather
changes—and that's enough. Other people I have
to have around or at the end of a phone line
or I begin crying like an infant in a crib alone
in a room at the end of a hall when the afternoon
shadows start. A headache tells you when there's
something wrong you should pay attention to.
So pay attention. Pain is intelligent. It's also
something you can switch off up to a point.
Some treatments require you to believe in them,
others just grab you by the ass. *Don't you believe
in medicine, Doctor? Don't you believe in justice,
Judge?* If it wasn't for film noir, I don't think
we'd take autumn like we do, letting it roll over us.
We'd grab our pitchforks and do something about it.
Which reminds me that I don't own a pitchfork.
Maybe that's been my problem. I own two leaf rakes,
both with warped teeth. One has blood on the handle
from when I went overboard raking this spring
and had to wear bandages on my hands for a week.
What do I need a pitchfork for, now I think of it?
I'm just now realizing how tough I really am.
It's two in the afternoon. The sky clouded over.
I'm going inside where it's warm to simmer in my
many strengths, to fry some bacon and check my email
three times in ten minutes to see if anyone loves me.

# One Theory of What's Happening Out There

I'm not calling you. You're not calling me.
We're emailing to ask whose turn is it
and the wolves are gathering in the ditches
of abandoned elementary school parking lots
to talk about us. They use human voices.
They speak with our voice boxes. We don't
know our voice boxes are gone. We're busy
roaming our shrinking backyards looking
for marbles left by children long ago. Like
water, a marble gets clean by being in dirt.
Rub the soil away and see a small clear idea.
Bring it to your eye; there's a whole world.
Cracks and pits for our landers to touch down.
Utilities are paid through the next month.
I'm not saying I have anything particularly
interesting to relate to you, or you to me.
But it's so far to the next planet. Bacteria
may be able to survive the journey. But
even then they'll have to burrow inside
the stones that fling themselves recklessly
through the distances between us.

# Where You and I Could Get a Coffee Sit by a Lake and Talk

At some point I was the only one I knew who could
drive and that's the way it was always going to be.
Then next thing I know everyone's got a license.
Things have been whizzing out of my control like that
ever since. I buy bananas and next thing I know
they're all black. I was sure I decided to eat those—
at least one a day. They're healthy and they're
radioactive. Don't try to figure that one out.
The dishwasher is peeling open the kitchen counter
from the steam it releases. It's like a dark grin slowly
widening at me when I approach the sink to wash
my hands approximately two-thirds more than
is reasonably necessary. When things are bad
I'll walk upstairs while I've already got my coat on
to check a fourth time the burners are off and
the toaster's unplugged. There was a girl in school
whose dad had died a long time ago. Now we're
all that girl. She watched public access TV shows
of marching bands on football fields with the sound
turned down—bright lights against a black sky.
I wanted to know people like that. Where are they
now? I've lost track of all the planets we've
discovered with liquid water, the moons cradling
geysers, moons of moons concealing lakes of
pearly liquid below the surface. The Earth-like
Earths strewn across the known cosmos that's just
a known cosmos. Planets with the possibility of
life on them. I'd like to live on one of those.

# But I Live Here (Empty Place)

I let out the last of my wolves so long ago
there's not even a smell left in the chute.
My backyard used to tipple and flounce,
but these days I'm pushing a cheddar
sandwich with a snapped broomstick
in case on the next time around it rouses.
At night the stars fall into the neighbor's pool
and frolic like children in an animated film
where they're more fun than actual children.
Over here, clumps of weeds by a brown bush
howling under the newly starless sky.
I walk over to them, expectant for once,
and they immediately stop. They seem
to look up at me as if I shouldn't be there.

# A Hole in the Sky Corresponding to One in Me

Great. The sun's finally out. I'm going
to sit here with my arms crossed
and let it burn the back of my neck.
Then I can be angry at an entire planet.
Heavenly body, whatever it is.
Pluto got hosed and I'm still miffed.
I need so much to help me get through.
It's not like I used Pluto every night—
but it was nice to know he was there.
Sure I know he remains in space but
it's not the same. In sixth grade I made
a rhyme with a line for every planet plus
the sun. It came to ten. An even number.
It all worked out. Now they keep
showing headlines with discoveries
about the surface—methane snow deep
across dark mountains—but it's too late.
I'm stuck here with twelve hundred
bucks work to be done to my car.
I was driving a death trap and didn't
know it. Today's headline: New Scans
Reveal Sealed Chambers Inside
King Tut Pyramid. Maybe his wife.
Maybe there's something in there
to help. They used to grind up mummies
as medicine. Imagine a mound of
gray powder in a spoon. Spin in
hot water—add lemon, honey—and
drink it. You have to be seriously
at the end of your options. I'd try it.

# Sneaking Back Inside

And with the new organizational system
for the closets we're finally going to get
our act together. I'm not looking so I'm not
seeing all the good stuff—my stuff—you're
throwing out in ways that make you feel
better and lighter and like you're living
the right life and which make me a little
sad because it's just more of things going
away never to return and if I get any lighter
I won't even be able to stay here on this planet.
I barely feel like I can right now, which is
why I love trees and dead cars in driveways.
We kept them on the edge of our driveway.
I don't know what the neighbors thought
and I don't care. I knocked a window out
by accident (sort of) playing with a slingshot
I shouldn't have. I snuck into my bedroom
when no one was looking and pretended
I'd been there all day. I lived in fear and
when nothing happened I stopped living in fear—
at least about that window. We taped it up
and on summer afternoons I'd lay across
the back seat reading novels listening to
the rain on the roof and basically what I'm
saying is do what you want with the closets.
I don't care. But if you see me later at the
side of the house going through the trash
it's because when I went to pull it down
the drive it felt so unusually heavy. I thought
there might be a body in there. Maybe mine.

# Throwing Pebbles into Perpetual Orbit

I love bats. It's safe to say we all do these days.
Vampires are real and deserve psychological counseling.
I shouldn't look at news because all I read are
headlines and make up the stories later in my head.
I love every glacier that ever scraped bare stone
and I've never seen a single one. I don't get out much.
Some days I can't afford a hot dog for lunch.
If you buy quality you don't have to worry what's inside.
The sound of a lone human coughing in a room at night
is as timeless as watching waves roll in or trying
not to see skulls in the campfire after everyone's asleep.
When I was young, my brothers would throw stones
at the stars to bring bats low. First the lob then wait
a second or two and down from dark branches
these black leather birds pass by so jerkily and swift
you couldn't get a clear image. My brothers were
ten feet tall then with arms like railroad ties.
The maples a thousand feet high—easily—and I
was a tiny person. I had mosquito repellant sprayed on
my knees by my mother. I was protected from everything.

# A Lot Going On up There

If anything seeing the hawk hovering
in the glass top patio table makes it
more majestic. The clouds a mattress
too far away to touch. I lean over,
the bird blotted out by my big fat head.
The doctor who caught me when first I fell
to earth remarked—*Baby got a big brain*.
I hope he had a nice house with a big pool,
his children bringing him bits of blue glass
found in the woods out back. I hope
they didn't experiment with huffing
as they hit puberty. If a Mylar balloon
landed in his backyard, did he check
the postcard in its sandwich bag:
Dear Whoever Finds This. My name
is Christopher Citro. I'm in second grade
and go to Gardner Elementary School.
My teacher is Mrs. Randall. This was
all her idea. I think she's unhappy at home.
The hawk moves out of the way to let
a little hot package of breath rise up
like a rocket and fall again like a rocket.
He's watching us with better eyes.
I make him out inside the patio table.
The sky is blue but a muted blue.

# On Our Mountain Made of Crushed Mountains

Merely a bowl of melon balls but
Julius Caesar can't eat them.
They beat the wooly mammoths
we'd all like a ride on. Last night
I watched the film right up to
my battery running out then shifted
my neck and watched the stars.
One light getting bigger. That's when
it's coming toward us. I was 10 when
we filled out the government UFO
form *a railroad lantern, revolving*
*jade lights. Held above the garden.*
*It didn't just leave. It removed itself.*
Whole communities still exist
with few or no words for numbers.
Perhaps they have *some* or *a couple*
but that's it. And these are intelligent
people. I let the bee get angry.
Shooed it out the door anyway
because an adult can handle that
sort of thing. I wanted to run away.
I'm a child inside an adult shell,
pulling levers, pushing buttons.
Sometimes it's quite frantic. Driving
in the city. Sometimes I'm petting
the knobs on their smooth heavy heads
when you're around, on the couch
with your legs drawn up. At some
point the last of the incandescents
will burn out and we'll be left
with LEDs or those snake-curled

fluorescents. We'll be living like
always but the light around us
will be completely different. Green
not golden. Teaspoons of heat
no longer rising from our lamps.
Our tongue touching the back of our lips
at even a photo of something good.

# We Are Many People Some Okay

Apparently you can rub your eyes too much—
since the doctor said to her yes you did and
here are drops and stop doing that. Part of me
thinks I'll make my eyes look older pulling down
the corners which I do when I've been staring
too long thinking the thoughts behind my usual
thoughts which just amount to now what have I
done. When I ask you not to stand there watching
me spoon potatoes from the steamer it's nothing
to do with you and I hope you believe that.
My mom is two inches tall and lives in one side
of my brain pressed between gray walls and she's
pissed. I get approximately ten seconds to do a job
right and then the yells. I'm ten years old. I can't
expect you to have noticed. It happens in an instant.
Then I grow back up again which means I try to
use my mouth to explain to you what's happening
and it's not your fault. I need you to understand
it's not your fault. The sky full of clouds
like old snow in road ruts. They're
clouds. They should never look that way.

# Right Like Yellow Along a Banana

The bird on the step is in shadow until
it twitches and suddenly parts of it are lit
a golden brown. Sometimes it's the tail,
sometimes the left half of beak and tail.
The clouds are rolling the wrong direction,
but I'm not going to be the one to say.
I had my usual nightmares last night, but
I'm not having one now, which I cling to
the way the atmosphere grips the earth.
Have you ever paid close enough attention
to the *whooshing* sound it makes rushing
into a vacuum-packed jar of peanuts?
When I woke this morning I immediately
felt pounds lighter. Upstairs on my side
of the bed now there's an impression
of me, dozens of pounds of meat-weight
pressing down that you can't see, but if
you place your hand there, you'll feel
the coolness of my absence. The bird
whose noise is making the noises
all the other birds do is behind me
in the cottonwoods above my shoulder.
Sunlight's landing on everything now,
my knees, my tea, the grass around me,
and it isn't making any noise as it hits,
not a plink, not a quiet little crush.

# Sunsets Like Strobe Lights

Sunrises like cars passing along the highway.
I'm with you. Let's live like we'll never end.
And this doesn't mean mountain climbing
without ropes or taking up the harder drugs
that turn you into a lizard. It means we'll
outlive the landlord and the landlord's kids
and inherit this rental via some archaic law
brought from Olde England where, by right of
sitting in the same place for so long and not
dying, this plot of land, this two car garage
with one rotting door is now ours. We're like
gods anyway, so a house of our own is fitting.
The blue moonlight. The short drive too hot
to walk barefoot in the summer to get the mail.
The dots on the bedroom ceiling that signify
something seeping in from the attic. If you
promise to never die, then I promise, too.
We'll go on eating off the same plates,
keeping the Thai restaurant on the corner
in business, in a never-ending wave of days.
We'll wash the marks left by our lips from
the edges of the mason jars until those jars
wear back into sand. Our lips left floating
in the salt air above a white beach, you and I
connected at either end and holding fast.

# Watching You to See How to React to All This

In the distance we're never sure just what are boats
and what might be birds. The sky and the horizon
meet in a line the eye loses if it doesn't hold fast.
The bravery it takes to be at the beach instead of
back home in the air conditioning. So much of this
is opening ourselves up. So much exposed skin,
the beautiful people and the lumpy people and
the children skittering about screaming at the sea
and smacking the sand with tiny shovels.
I am beautiful because I am here with you.
Light runs along my arms and falls onto the sand
where your toes are buried. When I look into
your eyes, I can see myself and I'm looking
not that bad. I smell like coconuts and I look like
one of those people who know what they're doing.
I have no idea what I'm doing. I could be at home
gluing together a model of this moment and doing it
all wrong, getting pieces stuck to my fingers,
considering sniffing the glue then wandering
into the backyard to watch strings from the sun fall
on me. For two hours. Then getting something to eat.

# Calling for One Another When We're Right There

You slicing scallions in another room,
a knife thump against a bamboo mat.
The record comes to an end, the needle
clicks back, and the world comes in.
Sometimes I'll remove a strip of light,
a hair from the corner of my mouth,
and run. Last night tasted toothpaste
in the corner of your lips as we rolled
together on the bed making each other
so violently thankful. How soon after
your breathing reached the deep pockets
of sleep, your long back pressed to me.
The night a sack we tip into, grab
what doesn't slip between our fingers
and push into our mouths so quick.
The plains below, bay trees shudder,
leaves flavoring the wind. Our tongues
tired now, rest in wet caves. The cedar
sprout you lifted from the garden
hours ago, a clot of needles atop a trunk
thin as a twist-tie, roots extending from
a single red chip of mulch like an egg.
Your closed eyes as I try to kiss
your lips and kiss your teeth instead.

# I Smell the Dirt All Around Me and Above

Let go and see where falling takes you. Here
I'm watching you chop carrots and there's all
these gold coins piling up beneath your fingers.
You're making me feel rich. I'm afraid to go
outside because then I will feel wet. Thus
the struggle on this winter morning. I woke
with Carlsbad Caverns in my skull but I'm
trying to move on. I've been to Mammoth
but never Carlsbad. I wrote a report on it
in sixth grade so I still own it inside.
I can go there when the wind blows.
One thing you don't get deep inside a cave
is a blizzard. The wax or ceramic bandits
wouldn't like it. Yes, the reference to
a cathedral. Yes, the antique helmets
with white fire for light. How ropes help
keep us alive. That almost imperceptible
thread into the darkness. Once I crossed
between tight rock walls—a long drop
and dark water beneath—duck-walking
my feet to either side, suspended thanks to
nothing but the pressure of myself pushing
outward. When someone loves me enough
to send a communication these days
I write or telephone right back.

# The Secret Lives of Little Girls

How loudly you can groan if you just use your eyes.
Children are adept at this, twelve year old girls especially.
Alone, high in mountain caves along cliff sides
accessible solely by toeholds and birds of prey,
they deflate and slouch a bit in ease.
At such times they might play jacks or jump a rope,
its woven line slapping the cave roof, freeing
gypsum flowers to flutter down in fragments
over reeking hides and doll parts piled in corners,
a sleeping area of matted glossy magazines,
a fire ring of rolled socks in particolored balls,
simple flint implements, a clamshell for stripping pelts,
small animal bones for holding a bow in the hair,
a pompom here and there caked with glitter and mud.
Hidden in the back beyond reach of firelight, a doll house—
perfectly split down the center as eggs rarely are—
where the gods live. The mommy god and the daddy god
stand facing each other either side of a four-poster bed,
a cellophane fire in the living room hearth below.
A dining room table set for three, three plates, three napkins,
and cutlery—a clear plastic goblet at each place.
In the daughter chair, an acorn balanced atop an acorn.
A smile scraped into the top one,
presumably by sharpened antler bone.

# We Give Ourselves New Medals (We Give Ourselves a Chance)

Sunshine breaks out in a bright yellow rash.
Garage sales have risen around us in the night
like termite mounds. As light crosses the sky
in its well worn groove, insects revolve
to keep in the shade. We're not fools here.
Have you been to the elementary school
open house? Our gas station sells soft serve
through a little window away from the pumps.
We're charged extra for paying with credit.
We're not happy about that, considering
stretching the man who owns the station
across a termite mound, candles burned just
to darken the wick jabbing him in the back.
But we will not, of course. We'll go inside.
There's supposed to be something good on TV.
A small girl in a toy convertible backs
across her lawn, over the curb, and out
to seek an inland route to the Pacific.

## We Were Doing Fine and Then We Disappeared Peacefully

One light in a field of others can easily get lost
unless it's moving. We're equipped to hunt rabbits,
so we can see the darting though now we live
off of steaks and salted caramel ice cream. We love
the sound of a train in the distance, possibly
because it might be a large animal leaving. I love
that there's a cave man inside you. Place my hand
where it should be. Leave the light on. We love
the way it flickers against the stone walls and
the cat poster. Excavations on our mattress
by those who come after will uncover, what—
flint implements, a cooking bowl with residue
from the last meal we left unfinished, so we
could roll into a ball together and bang against
the stalagmites and stalactites. The chimes
echo back into where we can't fit ourselves,
where the water comes sweet and good.

# These Seagulls Are Better More Gullier Than the Ones in the City

I don't know if the Great Lakes have tides or not.
No one tells me anything anymore. My dad said
always unplug an appliance before taking it apart.
I fix a lamp socket every few years and milk that
for all it's worth. We call it a *dad moment*
and the cat leaves the room shaking her head.
That way lies Canada. The people there are friendly
and have good healthcare. Up the shore to the east
is the nuke plant, so situate yourself on the rocks
so as not to see it. There. No more nuke plant.
To the west are ice cream stands and fish fry joints.
What more do we need in this life? Sometimes
the most effective procedure is to cut the head off
and pull the hook through. The barb makes trying
to yank it back out more destructive than just
accepting you're caught. Most fisherpersons carry
wire clippers in their tackle for just this reason.
I may not know everything about inland tides, but
I know they sell scents to spray on your lures for
the big ones—they do not call them *perfumes*,
they call them *attractants*—but I'm probably
going on too long at this point. See that white
fleck in the distance there? That's a sailboat.
It has everyone you love on it. They're eating
perch sandwiches and licking shaved lemon ices.
The captain has aimed the boat at you and
it's on its way. Hold my hand. I'm the captain's
helper and the boat's coming for me, too.

# Acknowledgments

My thanks to the editors of the following journals and anthologies where the following poems first appeared:

*Alaska Quarterly Review*: "In Small Significant Ways We're Horses," "To Keep At Least Partially in the Air" and "We Are Many People Some Okay"

*Blackbird*: "Anyway and Try to Stay Alive on What It Gives Us"

*Booth*: "Go On Take Another Little Piece of My Heart"

*The Carolina Quarterly*: "Sunsets Like Strobe Lights" and "That's Why They Invented Cheesecake"

*Cider Press Review*: "But I Live Here (Empty Place)"

*Collagist*: "Otherwise Inexplicable Animation to the Forms Above"

*Colorado Review*: "Shelter Awhile" and "Smell of Wet Earth Like the Inside of My Hands"

*Columbia Poetry Review*: "Bring Me with You"

*Columbia: A Journal of Literature and Art*: "So That's What an Invisible Barrier Looks Like"

*The Cortland Review*: "Calling for One Another When We're Right There"

*Crab Creek Review*: "You Can Keep Your Employee of the Month Award"

*Crazyhorse*: "These Seagulls Are Better More Gullier Than the Ones in the City"

*cream city review*: "Sneaking Back Inside" and "We Live on a Foreign Planet This One"

*Gulf Coast*: "If We Had a Lemon We'd Throw It and Call That the Sun"

*Hayden's Ferry Review*: "Save the Receipts for a Kind of Diary"

*Iowa Review* Blog: "We Might As Well Be Hovering"

*The Journal*: "Holding My Head in Both My Hands" and "We Were Doing Fine and Then We Disappeared Peacefully"

*The Laurel Review*: "Right Like Yellow Along a Banana" and "The Low Crumble of Distant Applause"

*The Los Angeles Review*: "How We Make It Home Eventually"

*Massachusetts Review*: "Yesterday I Saw a Small Snake Holding Still"

*Meridian*: "One Theory of What's Happening Out There" and "The Sky We Want to Reach Up and Press Our Thumbs Into"

*Mid-American Review*: "At First It Buzzed Then Even the Buzzing Stopped" and "One Light in a Field of Other Lights"

*The Missouri Review*: "Removing the Butter Dish from the Fridge with a Sense of Urgency," "Returning Home After the Funeral," "Sick of Sick," "Throwing Pebbles into Perpetual Orbit," "Watching You to See How to React to All This" and "Where You and I Could Get a Coffee Sit by a Lake and Talk"

*Narrative*: "A Lot Going On up There" and "To the Dirt Which Will in Time Consume Us All"

*North American Review*: "Bats and Applesauce" and "On a Foreign Planet Surrounded by Sugar Maples"

*Passages North*: "One Push on Top Is All It Takes"

*Phoebe*: "The Hay Out There and the Hay in You"

*Pleiades*: "I Smell the Dirt All Around Me and Above"

*Ploughshares*: "The People Who Live Near Us Are Our Neighbors"

*Poetry Northwest*: "We Give Ourselves New Medals (We Give Ourselves a Chance)" and "I'm Back Here I'm Paddling Too"

*Pool*: "A Mud Puddle Shaped Mud Puddle"

*Prairie Schooner*: "Creation Myth"

*Raleigh Review*: "Dear Diary Where Is Everybody," "Light at the Beach a Thousand Doctors" and "Waves Frozen Like Wrinkles on Dog Skin"

*Rattle*: "Our Beautiful Life When It's Filled With Shrieks" and "The Mutual Building"

*Redivider*: "Barely Managing the House Plants Thing"

*River Styx*: "We Come Here Every Day So You've Already Won"

*Salt Hill*: "You're Welcome to the Rest"

*Sixth Finch*: "The Sweet of Being Made Right"

*Southern Indiana Review*: "Beaver Lake" and "Elegy for the Travel Agents"

*The Southeast Review*: "An Emergency Every Day of the Week"
*Southwest Review*: "Shadows of Blackbirds on Our Arms"
*Subtropics*: "The Secret Lives of Little Girls"
*Sycamore Review*: "It's Something People in Love Do"
*Zone 3*: "On Our Mountain Made of Crushed Mountains"

"An Emergency Every Day of the Week" republished at Verse Daily (July 14, 2013 and July 8, 2014)

"Gathering a Few Facts" first published in the anthology *Best New Poets 2014: 50 Poems from Emerging Writers* (Samovar Press/Meridian, 2015)

"If We Had a Lemon We'd Throw It and Call That the Sun" republished in the anthology *New Poetry from the Midwest* (New American Press, 2020)

"It's Something People in Love Do" republished in the 2018 *Pushcart Prize Anthology* (Pushcart Press, 2018) and in the anthologies *A Constellation of Kisses* (Terrapin Books, 2019) and *Show Us Your Papers* (Main Street Rag, 2020)

"The Secret Lives of Little Girls" republished in the anthology *The Doll Collection* (Terrapin Books, 2016)

"Sick of Sick" republished in the anthology *Show Us Your Papers* (Main Street Rag, 2020)

"So That's What an Invisible Barrier Looks Like" received first place in the 2015 *Columbia: A Journal of Literature and Art* Poetry Competition as judged by Beth Ann Fennelly

"Go On Take Another Little Piece of My Heart" title inspired by "Piece of My Heart" composed by Jerry Ragovoy and Bert Berns and sung by Janis Joplin with Big Brother and the Holding Company.

ACKNOWLEDGMENTS

"How We Make It Home Eventually" epigraph from "Crystal Declension" by Charles Wright.

"Otherwise Inexplicable Animation to the Forms Above" title and italicized text from "Another Dimension: Reconsidering Picasso the sculptor" by Peter Schjeldahl (*The New Yorker*, September 21, 2015).

"Peaks Shot with Hairs of Lightning" title inspired by a line from *The Wrong Case* by James Crumley.

"Removing the Butter Dish from the Fridge With a Sense of Urgency" italicized text from *And Then There Were None*, directed by René Clair.

"Shelter Awhile" italicized text from "A Bit of Winding Road" by Mary Ruefle.

"So That's What an Invisible Barrier Looks Like" title inspired by a line from *Time Bandits*, directed by Terry Gilliam.


Most of these poems were written while listening to Lee Morgan's album *The Raja*, featuring Lee Morgan, trumpet; Hank Mobley, tenor saxophone; Cedar Walton, piano; Paul Chambers, bass; and Billy Higgins, drums. Boundless inspiration.

"Bats and Applesauce" is for J Keirn-Swanson.


Thank you to the editors of all the journals and anthologies where these poems have appeared—I am indebted to you for your support and for your occasional suggestions which have improved the work.

Thank you to the following magnificent people for your many considerations: the Citro family, the Ruhlen family, Alexander Weinstein, Phil Memmer, Georgia Popoff, Judy Carr, Steve Castro, Bob Early, Michael

Poore, Jason Jordan, Kevin Bertolero, Virginia Zech, Tony Ardizzone, Lee Upton, Traci Cox, Brian Daldorph, Grant Reeher, John Gallaher, Mark Montgomery, Richard Bower, Bill Henderson, Tom Hunley, Jazzy Danziger, Dorianne Laux, Mary Ruefle, and Beth Ann Fennelly.

Thank you to Molly Dumbleton, Jeffrey Meeuwsen, Amy Sinclair, Regin Igloria, and the Curational Board at Ragdale Foundation for awarding me a fellowship and the time and space to finalize this manuscript.

Thank you to my teachers whose past lessons continue to inspire me, including Wayne Dodd, Maura Stanton, Cathy Bowman, Maurice Manning, and Ross Gay.

Thank you to my colleagues and students at SUNY Oswego, The Downtown Writers Center in Syracuse, The Kettle Pond Writers' Conference, and The Martha's Vineyard Institute of Creative Writing.

Thank you to Dana Curtis for your kindness and for believing in my work.

Thank you to Ariana-Sophia Kartsonis for selecting this book to win the 2019 Antivenom Poetry Award.

Thank you to Amanda Friedman for allowing your luminous photograph to grace the cover.

Thank you to Ross Gay, Diane Seuss, Lee Upton, and Dean Young for the generosity of your words.

Thank you to Dustin Nightingale for your friendship, your poetic comradeship...for reading me poems over the phone at 4 in the morning.

Thank you to J Keirn-Swanson for your friendship, your steadfast support...for that time years ago when you asked me to reread you my poem while you went "Oh, man!" again and again.

And lastly and entirely thank you to Sarah Ruhlen, the inspiration for my best poems, my darling companion, my friend, my sweet, sweet love…the girl I most want to go sledding with at midnight drinking martinis out of sippy cups.

CHRISTOPHER CITRO is the author of *The Maintenance of the Shimmy-Shammy* (Steel Toe Books, 2015). His honors include a Pushcart Prize for poetry, *Columbia Journal*'s poetry award, and a creative nonfiction award from *The Florida Review*. His poems appear widely in literary magazines and journals such as *American Poetry Review, Ploughshares, Iowa Review, Gulf Coast,* and *Alaska Quarterly Review*. His writing has been anthologized in *Best New Poets 2014, New Poetry from the Midwest 2019,* and *Best Microfiction 2020*. He teaches creative writing at SUNY Oswego and lives in sunny Syracuse, New York.

# ELIXIR PRESS TITLES

**POETRY**

*Circassian Girl* by Michelle Mitchell-Foust
*Imago Mundi* by Michelle Mitchell-Foust
*Distance From Birth* by Tracy Philpot
*Original White Animals* by Tracy Philpot
*Flow Blue* by Sarah Kennedy
*A Witch's Dictionary* by Sarah Kennedy
*The Gold Thread* by Sarah Kennedy
*Rapture* by Sarah Kennedy
*Monster Zero* by Jay Snodgrass
*Drag* by Duriel E. Harris
*Running the Voodoo Down* by Jim McGarrah
*Assignation at Vanishing Point* by Jane
    Satterfield
*Her Familiars* by Jane Satterfield
*The Jewish Fake Book* by Sima Rabinowitz
*Recital* by Samn Stockwell
*Murder Ballads* by Jake Adam York
*Floating Girl (Angel of War)* by Robert
    Randolph
*Puritan Spectacle* by Robert Strong
*X-testaments* by Karen Zealand
*Keeping the Tigers Behind Us* by Glenn J.
    Freeman
*Bonneville* by Jenny Mueller
*State Park* by Jenny Mueller
*Cities of Flesh and the Dead* by Diann
    Blakely
*Green Ink Wings* by Sherre Myers
*Orange Reminds You Of Listening* by Kristin
    Abraham
*In What I Have Done & What I Have Failed
    To Do* by Joseph P. Wood
*Bray* by Paul Gibbons
*The Halo Rule* by Teresa Leo
*Perpetual Care* by Katie Cappello
*The Raindrop's Gospel: The Trials of St.
    Jerome and St. Paula* by Maurya Simon
*Prelude to Air from Water* by Sandy Florian
*Let Me Open You A Swan* by Deborah Bogen
*Cargo* by Kristin Kelly
*Spit* by Esther Lee
*Rag & Bone* by Kathryn Nuerenberger

*Kingdom of Throat-stuck Luck* by George
    Kalamaras
*Mormon Boy* by Seth Brady Tucker
*Nostalgia for the Criminal Past* by Kathleen
    Winter
*I will not kick my friends* by Kathleen Winter
*Little Oblivion* by Susan Allspaw
*Quelled Communiqués* by Chloe Joan Lopez
*Stupor* by David Ray Vance
*Curio* by John A. Nieves
*The Rub* by Ariana-Sophia Kartsonis
*Visiting Indira Gandhi's Palmist* by Kirun
    Kapur
*Freaked* by Liz Robbins
*Looming* by Jennifer Franklin
*Flammable Matter* by Jacob Victorine
*Prayer Book of the Anxious* by Josephine Yu
*flicker* by Lisa Bickmore
*Sure Extinction* by John Estes
*Selected Proverbs* by Michael Cryer
*Rise and Fall of the Lesser Sun Gods* by Bruce
    Bond
*Barnburner* by Erin Hoover
*Live from the Mood Board* by Candice Reffe
*Deed* by Justin Wymer
*Somewhere to Go* by Laurin Becker Macios
*If We Had a Lemon We'd Throw It and Call
    That the Sun* by Christopher Citro
*White Chick* by Nancy Keating

**FICTION**

*How Things Break* by Kerala Goodkin
*Juju* by Judy Moffat
*Grass* by Sean Aden Lovelace
*Hymn of Ash* by George Looney
*Nine Ten Again* by Phil Condon
*Memory Sickness* by Phong Nguyen
*Troglodyte* by Tracy DeBrincat
*The Loss of All Lost Things* by Amina Gautier
*The Killer's Dog* by Gary Fincke
*Everyone Was There* by Anthony Varallo
*The Wolf Tone* by Christy Stillwell